Somerton, Ilchester and Langport

IN OLD PHOTOGRAPHS

Overt Locke during service with the Royal Garrison Artillery in the First World War, which included the Battles of Ypres and the Somme. He started the well-known family business in 1925 in the West Street premises that it still occupies today. The firm began as an ironmonger and builders' merchant, and later became a Texaco oil distributor. Overt was a magistrate and, during the Second World War, chief of the Somerton Fire Brigade in which the Locke family always had a special interest. He was succeeded in the business by his brother Dennis and then his son Alan, the well-known Somerton historian, who is the present managing director.

Somerton, Ilchester and Langport

IN OLD PHOTOGRAPHS

Collected by GERALD GOSLING
and FRANK HUDDY

Alan Sutton Publishing Limited
Phoenix Mill . Far Thrupp
Stroud . Gloucestershire

First published 1993

For our daughters, Sarah, Nola and Georgia

British Library Cataloguing in Publication Data

A catalogue record for this book is available from
the British Library

ISBN 0-7509-0395-3

Typset in 9/10 Sabon.
Typesetting and origination by
Alan Sutton Publishing Limited.
Printed in Great Britain by
Redwood Books, Trowbridge.

Contents

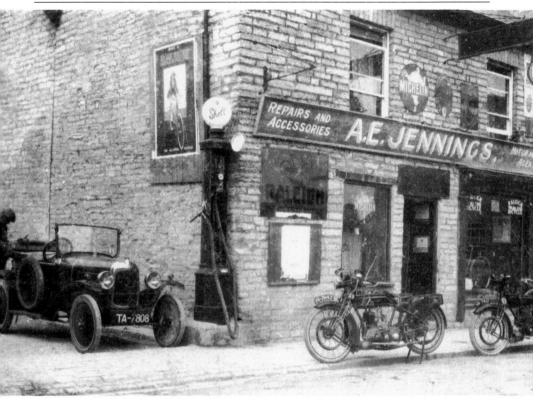

A.E. Jennings, motor and cycle repairs and accessories shop, West Street, Somerton, *c.* 1920. Note the Shell petrol pump, the first one in the town. One might well wonder exactly where the storage tank to the pump was situated, even in such happier days when the world was not quite so overburdened with regulations. Such pumps had been introduced into Britain by the AA in the face of protests by the petrol companies, who claimed that their product was better sold in cans. Once it was seen they were wrong, pumps sprang up everywhere and the AA, who had only opened a few filling stations to prove a point, quietly faded out of the picture. Today these premises are occupied by an estate agent.

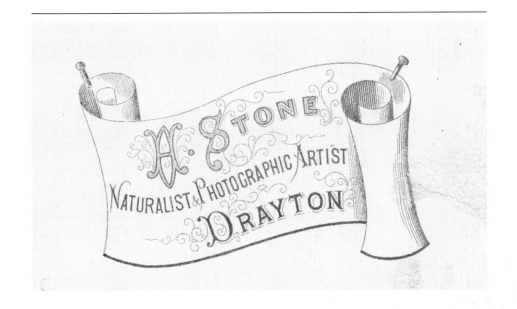

Introduction

Few people would consider themselves interested in matters relating to the past; yet my fifty years of amateur study of events local to the Langport and Huish Episcopi areas have left me in no doubt that factors that have affected one's neighbourhood in fact provide widespread pleasure.

The close research of documents and the continuous quest for yet more pieces of the historical jigsaw regarding one's parish may well be the domain of the few. Similarly, an archaeological dig can be a dirty and back-breaking pursuit, while local history books, many out of print, are expensive and often difficult to obtain, and the messages from both sources require disciplined study, which only a few people are prepared to undertake. However, if you mention activities of a deceased personality, an unusual feature of a demolished building or the degree of truth in a local legend, most folk will happily join your conversation and opinions will flow readily.

An early educational dictum claims firmly that Eyegate is more effective than Eargate. Certainly this truth is borne out by the popularity of books of old photographs, within which intriguing and often lost features of our past spring to life in well-presented form, using carefully reproduced copies of, in many cases, the sole remaining records of the locality, perhaps wisely saved by an enthusiast from a clearing-out bonfire. Thus readers may immerse themselves in some forgotten scenes upon which their forebears regularly cast their eyes, an exercise made possible by the dedicated and combined efforts of the collector and publisher.

Perhaps of unusual interest in this volume are a few pictorial reminders of floods in the Langport area, which are now much less frequent and widespread. These provide a flashback to a time of almost constant inundation, by both salt and fresh water, of the Somerset lowlands, when we had yet to take the painfully slow steps towards controlling the ravages of liquid nature on the local landscape.

Alan Sutton Publishing has now produced over three hundred titles in the Britain in Old Photographs series. Gerald Gosling and Frank Huddy's *Somerton, Ilchester and Langport* is well up to the publisher's high standard and the compilers deserve every success.

Brian Denman, Yeovil, 1993

SECTION ONE

Somerton

The Half Moon Inn and Tom Coggan's house, West Street, Somerton. Both were demolished to make room for the new railway line in 1906. The inn was rebuilt a few yards along the road.

The Triangle, Somerton. The Star inn is on the left, the delicatessen shop next door is now a private house and Maurice Newman's shop has also closed.

The Sir Edward Hext Almshouses, West Street, Somerton, c. 1900. The almshouses were built in 1626. There were eight of them at this time, but subsequently each pair was converted into a single dwelling (see opposite). The thatched house to the left is now Overt Locke's shop.

£1 REWARD

The above Reward will be paid to anyone giving information that will lead to the conviction of any person, or persons, who may be known to have broken the windows or otherwise damaged the Men's Almshouses in West Street, Somerton.

Information to be given to
Sergt. OVENDEN, Police Station, Somerton.

By order of the Trustees.

MABEL TAYLOR, Clerk.

J. G. WILLIAMS, THE PRINTERY, SOMERTON.

Vandalism is not always a product of the modern age.

The Sir Edward Hext Almhouses, West Street, Somerton, *c*. 1948.

Somerton Football Club, *c.* 1958.

Somerton Football Club, league champions, 1946–7. The man in 'civvies' (on goalkeeper Jim Pike's right) is Bill Wyatt, a former Crystal Palace and Yeovil Town player. With him are his brothers, Fred and Roy, Vic Lawrence and 'Chelsea' Wilcox.

Somerton Cricket Club, *c.* 1925. The club's ground in those days was where today's Fairfield and Montclefe Playing Fields are situated. Members here include Percy Edwards, landlord of the Globe, and Arthur Bond, the secretary.

Somerton Cricket Club, *c.* 1910. Back row, left to right: -?-, George Sweet, Walter Sweet, W.G. Longmire, -?-, Bruce Ayes, Walter Mundy. Front row: Billy Harding, Jim Pinney, Dickie Needham, Hall Stevenson, Arthur Shave, Pretor Pinney, Cyril Ford.

Somerton's old fire engine. This Ford is thought to have been brought from Bovey Tracey, *c*. 1938. Among the crew are Overt Locke, Mr Pinkhead, Mr Holland, Fred Cox, Courtney Locke and Dennis Locke.

Somerton Council road workers, 1926. Left to right: Harold Strang, Bill Hunt, Bill Kiddle, Bill Brown (behind), Ted Richards, Ted Castle.

Somerton British Legion Band, *c.* 1938. The members include Ted Squire, Reg Payne, Mr Plowman (bass drum) and Cliff Pattemore.

Somerton British Legion Band on parade, 1950s.

Digging the foundations of the milk factory at Somerton, *c.* 1920. The factory, then part of Cow & Gate, was badly bombed during the Second World War when nine of the workforce were killed and many others injured. The factory was never reopened and today the premises are a Somerset County Council depot.

Workers at the site of the milk factory, Somerton, *c.* 1920.

Frank Pattemore at Somerton Tythe Barn, *c.* 1930. The barn, like its parent farm, has been developed into houses.

Frank Brown, owner of the North Street Guernsey Dairy, early 1920s. He and Hettie Davey are in the aptly named Cow Square at his Donisthorpe premises. The dairy enjoyed a reputation for quality in the Somerton area. The Ford van was his first venture into mechanized deliveries. Note the milk bottles and cow on the pillars at the entrance to the dairy.

Somerton Motor Club members at a meeting at Chard, *c.* 1958. Those present include Dave Jenkin, Dave Pengelly, Brian Trott, Bunny Lukins, Gerald Thorn, Bobby Lukins, Brian Cooper, Mike Cooper, Roger Francis, Terry Cox, Philip Jenkin and the well-known Chard celebrity Jack Baulch, whose sporting interests included Chard Town and Yeovil Town Football Clubs and, of course, Chard Motor Club.

Somerton Motor Club, winners of the SW Centre Team Championship held at Chard, 1962. The members pose around Terry Cox's 500cc Triumph. Left to right: Eddie Trott, Bernie Singleton, Terry Cox, Bryan Goss, Dave Jenkin (team manager).

Somerton Supply Stores, Broad Street, Somerton, *c.* 1920. The stores were owned by Mr E.W. Raymont at this time. Later a Mr Gardiner bought the business, which is now a carpet shop.

Staff of Overt Locke at the firm's West Street premises. Those present include Leslie Sweet, Norma Shire, Mr and Mrs Overt Locke, Mr Matthews and Albert Bartlett.

Somerton Motor Club's first annual dinner at the Red Lion Hotel, Somerton, *c.* 1955. Among the members and guests are Garth Jotcham, Derek Stark, Harold Wells, Dave Jenkin, Fred Samways, Phil Cooper, Gerry Parker, Len Sanders, Des Penney, Wally Bowers and Peggy Lawrence.

Somerton Friendly Society Band outside the Old Hall, Somerton, *c.* 1905. The man on the left is thought to be Dr Valentine who lived in the Hall. Others present include Tom Coggan, Alfred Bowden and Mr Male.

The Red Lion Hotel, Somerton, 1922. The hotel was at this time in the hands of William George Longmire. In the arched entrance to the stables are, left to right: William Longmire, Percy Turner, 'the Boots', Bill junior (his son), Louise (his wife), Blanche (his sister).

The junction of the Sutton and Langport roads, Somerton, 1904. The curious combination of a cycle and fancy goods shop became a wet fish shop, run for many years by Ron Cooper. Today it is Tony's fish and chip shop.

Huish Grammar School football team, 1951–2.

Houses in West Street, Somerton, prior to being demolished when the new London–Castle Cary–Taunton line was built in 1906. The old Unicorn Hotel is in the background and the Half Moon Inn still exists.

'The Somerton Famous Circus' entry in the Somerton Carnival, 1932. Maurice Abbot is the bystander (far left), Eric Booth is on the horse (Queenie), the lovely ladies are, back row, left to right: Mrs Matthews, Mrs Cottam, Miss Lefort. Front row: M. Geard, W. Sweet, A. Wainwright.

Another entry at the Somerton Carnival, 1932. This bevy of lovely (their words, not ours) ladies came from Somerton Tennis Club. Back row, left to right: Mr Abbot, Mr Edwards, Mr Saunders, Mr Edwards, Mr P. Brown, Alan Northover and Phil Longmire. The fairy is Mrs P. Hooper.

Yeovil & District Co-operative Society Ltd, West Street, Somerton, *c.* 1934. Today a launderette occupies this site.

Broad Street, Somerton, *c.* 1902. The pub (right) became a beer shop, then in around 1945 Davis's builders office, but that too has gone. The taller building next door was Carter's collar factory.

Oliver Dean and his sons, Stan and Jim, outside the family carpentry and undertaker's business at Pould Pool. Formerly Oliver had been in New Street where his father was a blacksmith.

Ord, Battiscombe & Elwes Somerton Brewery's delivery lorry, probably pre-1914. It is popularly supposed that the driver is Mr Elwes himself. The brewery closed in 1920.

One of four jugs made by Mr John D. Pountney, the founder of the Bristol Potteries, and presented to members of Somerton Club in 1826 to be used on Club days. It is twelve inches high and a maximum of forty inches wide. Discovered in a Bristol antique shop in 1932, it is now back in Somerton in private hands.

Market Place, Somerton, c. 1898. Chard's boot shop (centre background) was demolished in the 1920s for road widening. The centre house, now an office equipment shop, remains. Lloyds Bank occupies the shop on the far right. The main interest here is the tiny window, 'King John's Window', in the side of the White Hart. It is so called because it is said that the French King John was imprisoned there, but there is no historical basis for this legend.

Arthur Evans, saddler and harness-maker, Somerton, *c.* 1908. Today this shop is a private house. Note the rabbits hanging on the extreme right.

Chard's boot shop (see opposite), shortly before it was demolished. Note the Globe and White Hart standing almost cheek by jowl with one another.

The Wings For Victory Parade procession passing through Somerton Market Place, *c.* 1943. The lady in front of the nurses is thought to be Mrs Street, A.G. Street's sister-in-law.

Somerton Fire Brigade and their engine, *c.* 1941. This is of special interest because it shows the former fire chief, Tom Coggan (background, far left) and his successor Overt Locke (left). There are three members of the Locke family on parade, three Hollands and Fred and Gerald Cox.

Dedication of the war memorial, Somerton, 1921.

An unknown all-male occasion and to an unknown destination, *c.* 1921. Among the Somerton men off for the day in one of Barlow Phillips' (Yeovil) charabancs are Jessie Hunt (parish clerk), Tom Coggan (who seems to pop up in every picture taken in Somerton at this time), Arthur Sweet, Mr Brown, Overt Locke, Fred Locke and Fred Cox.

Broad Street, Somerton, *c.* 1900. The Free Grammar School, established in 1670, is on the right. The trees in this street were planted to commemorate the wedding of the Prince of Wales, later Edward VII.

Somerton tended to look down on Langport, despite its near neighbour's importance as both a canal- and rail-head. The rivalry was underlined, on the cricket field at least, when the Somerton club went to the trouble of having a card, in the form of a skit on the Ashes, specially printed when, on 16 August 1913, they won by sixty-nine after dismissing Langport for thirty-two runs. Cyril Ford and Bill Longmire sit on guard beside a scuttle of real ashes. Wars have been fought for less!

Inside the old printing works, New Street, Somerton, 1902. The premises are still engaged in the printing trade today.

Cable & Wireless built the radio station at Badgers Cross, near Somerton, 1926. At this time it was nearing completion.

Workers at Somerton Laundry, New Street, *c.* 1918.

A carrier outside Somerton's Red Lion Hotel, *c.* 1896. It had a grey lead horse so that people approaching at night were better able to see it in the dark. When there was only a pair of horses, the outside horse was, if possible, lighter in colour. The handsome lion behind has long-since gone.

The Market Place, Somerton, *c.* 1920. The main point of interest here is the old brewery tower and chimney in the background.

Broad Street, Somerton, *c.* 1936. Bill Lidbury's hairdressers is on the left.

E. Withecombe & Son, butchers, Somerton, *c.* 1924. Today these premises, which were previously owned by Jack Morrish, are occupied by a bookshop. Withecombe's van has been decorated for the local carnival.

Brooking's butchers, West Street, Somerton, *c.* 1910. The modern butchers on the same site would be frowned on by today's health inspectors if they exposed their wares to the air, flies and passing dogs in this fashion.

Brooking's butchers' delivery cart, *c.* 1910.

Somerton postmen outside the Old Hall, Cow Square, *c.* 1935. Left to right: -?-, Bert Rolls, Mr Williams (postmaster), -?-, Charles Lawrence, -?-, Mr Pinkhead, Mr Easton, Harry Brown, Mr Smith. The building on the left is now a clothes shop.

The old tollhouse at Cary Bridge on the old turnpike road, near Somerton, *c.* 1890. The building has long-since been demolished.

Erleigh, Somerton, *c.* 1904. Now known as The Randle, this is an early nineteenth-century building and was once the home of the Pinney family.

The Blue Tea Rooms, Somerton, *c.* 1910. Built in 1550, these premises are still used as a cafe, now known as the Market House Cafe.

Tom Coggan's tailors, West Street, opposite the Hext Almshouses, *c.* 1905. Today this is a sweet shop.

West Street, Somerton, looking west, *c.* 1935. Shops tended to stay in one pair of hands much longer in the earlier years of the twentieth century. Mundy's cycle shop (right) is now an estate agents.

North Street, Somerton, *c.* 1905.

SECTION TWO

Ilchester

St Andrew's church, Northover, near Ilchester, *c*. 1924.

The Street, Northover, near Ilchester, *c.* 1920. Jim and Bessie Ireland are talking to Mr Oliver.

The Pepper Box Restaurant, Ilchester, *c.* 1950. Later known as the Wimpy Restaurant, this distinctive building is now empty and awaiting redevelopment.

The Waterfall, Northover, near Ilchester, *c.* 1909. Actually a weir on the River Yeo, this was removed in the 1920s and it is difficult today to find anyone who can remember seeing it.

The Square, Ilchester, *c.* 1924. Note the ivy on the Ivelchester Hotel.

Bird's (Yeovil) charabanc on an Ilchester outing to Cheddar, *c.* 1922. Will Masters is the driver. There can hardly be a town between, say, Exeter and Salisbury or Gloucester and Weymouth that does not have a similar picture taken outside Gough's Cave (see pages 116 and 133) where a resident, professional photographer plied his (considerable) trade.

Church of England Temperance Society, West Street, Ilchester, 1895. The fact that the members appear to be leaving the King William Inn is purely coincidental.

The Bath & Wells Church Army Waggon, Market Hill (renamed The Square by the bus company), Ilchester. Around the turn of the twentieth century, this vehicle was a regular visitor. The words 'Bath & Wells' had no connection with the Church of England diocese of that name. The Church Army's headquarters were in London, and they too divided up the country into 'parishes'.

The Bull Hotel, Ilchester, *c.* 1930. This hotel still exists, albeit much renovated.

High Street, Ilchester, looking south, *c.* 1938. Pickfords drapers, the Town Hall, Barnes Garage and the Dolphin Hotel are all visible.

Ilchester Cricket Club, *c*. 1952. Back row, left to right: -?-, -?-, -?-, Bob Hillier, -?-, Keith Smart. Front row: Dennis Evans, Ron Stevens, Sid Rice, Maurice Stevens, Wilf Coombes.

Ilchester cricketers during the tea interval, *c*. 1936. Back row, left to right: Arthur Davis (umpire), Gerald Masters, ? Loder, Alfie Cox, Jim Acort, Walt Vincent. Among those sitting are Wilf Coombes, Jack Coombes, Ken Masters, Owen Masters, 'Curly' Freestone, Clifford Cox and Mr Cornick.

Ilchester Home Guard, *c.* 1942. Roy Masters, Owen Freestone and Mr Huxtable at a gas-alert practice outside Guppy's bakery, Market Hill (now The Square).

Ilchester 'Militia' outside the Cow Inn, Limington Road, *c.* 1942. In the foreground are, left to right, Maurice Stevens, ? Avery, George Masters. Charlie Elford's milk float is in the background.

Ilchester Infants School (for four- to seven-year-olds), 1904. The mistress on the left is Annie Beale. Among the pupils are Frank Stevens, Esse Masters and a Miss Pope.

Ilchester School (for seven-year-olds and above), 1934. Back row, left to right: -?-, Kenneth Masters, -?-, Ted Ireland, ? Cornick, -?-. Front row: -?-, George Rodber, George Stevens, Gilbert Masters, -?-.

Church Street, Ilchester, looking north, *c*. 1895. The only vehicle in view on this road (one day to be the busy A303 West Country trunk road) is the pram outside the post office.

Church Street, Ilchester, looking north, *c*. 1920. The Cow Inn is now appropriately known as Bos House, 'bos' being a West Country word for cow, viz Boscastle or Bos Hill near Seaton.

The Barton, Ilchester, *c.* 1895. These houses (see below) were demolished in the 1960s and an Ilchester cheese factory (now closed) built in their place.

The Barton, Ilchester, seen from the church tower, *c.* 1895.

The first car in Ilchester at the turn of the twentieth century. This vehicle was owned by Dr Sequira, who lived and practised at Northover Manor for twenty-one years.

Dr Sequira with his wife and two daughters, *c*. 1930.

Ilchester Almshouses, *c.* 1893. All of those present are men, with the possible exception of the face peering from behind in the doorway.

Empire Day celebrations at Ilchester School, *c.* 1925. Among the pupils are Owen Masters, May Gillard and Percy Merrett. The school is now closed and new schools have been built at the opposite end of the village. In view of their War of Independence, American readers may be surprised to see the Stars and Stripes on display.

Ilchester VJ celebrations, August 1945. Lyndel Masters, with the flag, is leading the parade from Northover, over the bridge and into the town.

Widening Ilchester Bridge, *c.* 1925. The motor car brought growing importance to such roads as the A303 and, even if the vast majority of roadworks had to wait for a world war before getting under way, an effort to improve things is being made here.

Church Street, Ilchester, looking towards Yeovil, *c.* 1900. The post office and police station (right) are now private houses.

High Street, Ilchester, looking north, *c.* 1956. The A303 is still fairly deserted (but see page 55).

Dan Gillingham, Ilchester, *c.* 1930. Dan, a baker of some repute, had a shop in High Street.

Easton's grocery shop, High Street, Ilchester, *c.* 1925. The 'Today's Specialities' board on the right has both apples and cucumbers at sixpence per dozen and bananas at a shilling for seven. The shop has moved next door (right) and these premises are now a private house.

High Street, Ilchester, *c.* 1952. By this time the A303 had become a pedestrian's nightmare in high summer.

Ilchester Men's Club dinner, *c.* 1952. Front row, left to right: Don Banfield, Ern Abbott, 'Lefty' Burt. Others include George Bond, Reg Martin, Esse Masters, Dave Baker, 'Curly' Freestone, Fred Hubbard, Charles Bishop, Gerald Masters and John Critched. It was an all-male occasion. The ladies at the front belong to Harry Virgin's concert party, while those at the rear are waitresses.

Ilchester British Legion (the Royal came later), Women's Section, *c.* 1943. Members present for an unknown occasion include Marjorie Masters, Mabel Pope, Mrs Hann, Mrs Parker, Mrs Stuart, Peggy Wills, Kath Merrett, 'Granny' Merrett and Solly Clarke.

High Street, Ilchester, looking south, *c.* 1932. The post office is now the museum.

SECTION THREE
Langport

The Hanging Chapel (see page 66) between Langport and Huish Episcopi, 1960. This is the best-known and probably the most photographed building in the area. Usually the view is of the chapel, but this superb study of the beech trees in winter by the well-known local photographer, Keith Markham of Drayton, is taken from underneath the chapel. The thatched house is now tiled and the police station has moved.

Langport Congregational church fête at Brooklands, 26 June 1965. Elizabeth and Judith Webb, winners of the first and second prizes in the Original Hat Competition. The hats are made of bread baked by their father Douglas Webb, the well-known Langport baker.

Langport Post Office, Bow Street, pre-1910. This is now the site of Lloyds Bank and Challis's grocers. Sadly, the old pump (left) was demolished by a runaway lorry in 1910 and never replaced.

Cheapside, Langport, 1923, during the visit of Captain Twose, VC. The whole town has been decked out and everyone, including the now sadly defunct town band, has turned out to greet the local hero.

Viaduct under construction. Before the Langport East station and the new London–Castle Cary–Taunton line was opened in 1906, much work had to be done to provide fifty-foot-deep foundations for the viaduct over the North Street Moor.

The last meeting of the Langport Board of Guardians at the workhouse, 31 March 1930. The workhouse, which adjoined Union Drove at the top of Picts Hill, was built in 1842 to hold three hundred inmates. Among the Guardians are Mr W. Rolfe, Mr Crossman, F.C.P. Avis, Mr Lydford, Mr Phineus Winter Webb, Mr H.J.Denman, Mrs James Kelway and Mr E.Q. Louch.

Langport WI Choir, Bath, 1956. Back row, left to right: M.F. Williams, P. Coate, G. Miller, B. Eager. Middle row: J. Hussey, L. Butler, O. Mould, S. Scriven, D. Langridge, D. Binder, ? Pitman. Front row: A. Ridewood, M. Wastridge, ? Dabinett, L. Suter, M. Webb, D. Rouse, B. Gaurd, A. Priddle.

Langport Platoon Home Guard, *c.* 1941. Back row, left to right: -?-, Bill Wainright, Harry Willmott, Charlie Scriven, Fred Cox, Reg Cox, Henry Crocker, Reg Suter. Second Row: ? Lewis, Dennis Lock, Hubert Cox, Ashton Knight, Fred Cornelius, Ted Pavey, Bruce Cox, Ernie Walters. Third Row: Ray Reading, Wally Mitchell, Jack Cullen, Ted Lockyer, Fred Parker, Albert Cullen, Jack Squire, Harold Martin, Albert Jones. Front Row: Bert Davis, Fred Clark, Bill Loman, Capt. H.G. Jefferies, Major R.M. McEvoy, Eddie Martin, Les Hector, Charles Burt, W. Rouse.

The gardening staff at Hurds Hill, *c.* 1890. Mr Davidge (with the old-fashioned pruning knife) is in the centre and Tom Stacey (head gardener) on the far left. Note the almost obligatory watch and chain, even with working clothes, and the lawn mower.

The staff at Hurds Hill, Langport, *c.* 1900. The importance of the 'big house' to any rural community's economic life can be seen from the number of people employed by even such a 'small' place as Hurds Hill; and this group only includes Tom Stacey (head gardener) out of a staff of at least five outdoor workers (see above). Mrs Cox (the cook) is one of the magnificently dressed ladies at the front.

Bow Street, Langport, 1894. This street was prone to flooding. Outside the United Reformed church (1828), behind the wall on the right, Mr Gaylard (left) and Mr Cattle and his family are making their way through the waters. What was the photographer standing in?

Another flood in Bow Street, Langport, c. 1890. Note the flood boards in the first door on the left. Chant's chemist on the right has been an unoccupied, small shopping precinct for some years.

The staff at Langport West station enjoy a paddle, *c.* 1914.

P.W. Webb & Son, 'Bakers & Confectioners', Bow Street, Langport, *c.* 1945. Staff pose behind a new van. Left to right: Norman Webb, Reg Webb, Herbert Webb, Mrs Hall (the new assistant), Elsie Webb.

P.W. Webb & Son, Bow Street, Langport, 1935. Like the rest of the town, the well-known Langport bakers shop was well decorated for the Silver Jubilee of King George V.

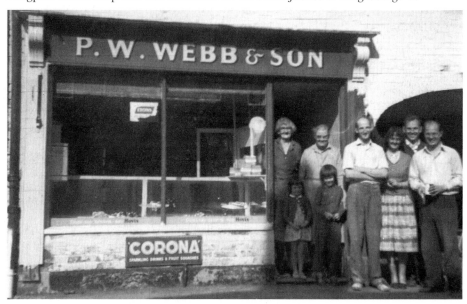

P.W. Webb & Son, Bow Street, Langport, 3 October 1964. On this day the business closed. Back row, left to right: Elsie Kirkby, Margorie Webb, Victor Crumb, Margaret Webb, Douglas Webb, Robert Webb. Front row: Judith Webb, Elizabeth Webb.

The Hanging Chapel (see page 57), Langport, from the west, *c*. 1910. This is one of the most interesting buildings in Langport. Dating from the fourteenth century, it has been used in turn as the Chantry of the Blessed Mary of Langport Eastover (i.e. on the east side of the River Parrett), a town hall (briefly from around 1575), the Grammar School (1706–90), an arms depot, a museum, a Sunday School, and, from 1891, has been the home of the Portcullis Masonic Lodge. Although it gives the impression of 'hanging' above the road, it is commonly said that it takes its name from the fact that three men were hanged nearby after Judge Jeffreys's Bloody Assizes in the wake of Monmouth's Rebellion in 1685. Today the ivy is no longer there, which is, perhaps, a pity.

The Dolphin Hotel (built in 1778), Bow Street, Langport, *c.* 1906. Its sign has long-since gone.

Bow Street, Langport, *c.* 1895. Although this postcard was postmarked 1910, the pinafore dresses and breeches worn by the children allow this picture to be dated some fifteen years before, but no earlier. Phineus Winter Webb is standing in the doorway of the bakers he opened *c.* 1894. Next to it is Chard's shoe shop and then the Spread Eagle Inn. Phineus was a member of the Town Trust, the body responsible for Langport's civil affairs after it ceased to be a borough in 1883. The cottage (in the background, immediately behind the gas light) was demolished in the 1920s.

Bow Street, Langport, *c.* 1908.

Bow Street, Langport, looking east, *c.* 1949. This street may have been built on the old Roman causeway, which might explain its arrow-straight path. The Dolphin Inn (built in 1778) still exists, but the local branch of the Yeovil & District Co-operative Society disappeared in the late 1970s to make room for the Moor Park development.

Bow Street, Langport, 1948. These four eighteenth-century cottages, which had been demolished by 1951, had a central passage providing access to a long-demolished row of similar cottages at the rear. These formed one of several 'courts' in the area, some of the houses being bargee dwellings. The step-down entrances were of no use in the floods to which the area was prone. These were superseded by 'two-step' entrances. The store (beyond the telegraph pole) was known as 'Holey House' because it was constructed of perforated bricks.

The staff of Phineus Winter Webb's bakery, *c.* 1900s. The business was opened in Bow Street, Langport, *c.* 1894. It stayed in the family's hands until closing in 1964. Among the workforce is Harry Jeanes.

Russell Barrington's carriage and pair, *c.* 1905. Russell (1840–1916) resided at Hurds Hill House. This was also the one-time residence of Walter Bagehot (1826–77), the famous economist who, among other things, advised Disraeli's government on the purchase of the Suez Canal.

Samuel Eli Scott, landlord of The Rose & Crown inn (see page 121), Huish Episcopi, *c.* 1958. In his role as governor of the local primary school he is presenting a Langport Road Safety Award. Also present are Dave Jenkin (Somerton Motor Club, second left), Ron Jotcham (behind Mr Scott) and Mr Stuckey (Langport Road Safety Officer, far right).

Presentation to Mr C. Coate, Langport postmaster, *c.* 1952. Mrs Coate is on the left. Among others present are M. Bown, E. Weatherall, P. Trott and H. Passmore.

North Street Council (now Primary) School, Langport, June 1922. Back row, left to right: M. Hussey, V. Martin, K. Gaylard, -?-, C. Hole, G. Jeanes, -?-, R. Miller. Front row: D. Woods, W. Long, R. Kite, G. Case.

North Street Council School, c. 1928. Back row, left to right: C. Cox, H. Wheller, -?-, H. Keirle, J. Lock, ? Cook, P. Trott, F. Hussey. Second row: D. Overd, M. Hussey, A. Parker, B. Lake, I. Boobyer, J. Long, ? Miller, I. Stacey, B. Chard, Smith. Third row: M. Short, R. Purchase, B. Medway, R. White, G. Kite, K. Gaylard, J. West, F. Payne, E. Boobyer. Front Row: -?-, ? Wheadon, W. White, D. Woods, G. Jeanes, M. Keivil, P. Pearce, D. Atyeo.

Harvest Home Sale, Langport, September 1963. Left to right: Revd H.O. Williams, John Butler (behind), Norman Butler, Douglas Webb, Stuart Matthews, Mr Hussey.

Langport Ladies Choir with their conductor Ashton Knight, *c.* 1955. Members present include Lilian Butler, Marina Standen, Mrs Rouse, Veronica Wood and Beryl Denman.

The Parrett Vale Choral Society and the Langport WI Choir combine at a social, Langport, 1963. Back row, left to right: Mr E. Scott, Dr Hanlon, Douglas Webb, Margaret Webb, John Butler. Middle row: Miss Babstock, Mrs Hanlon, Mrs Grinter, Mrs Rawlinson, Miss Denman, Miss Parker, Mrs Gourd, Miss R. Cull, Mrs Lock, Mrs Honey, Mrs Binder, Miss G. Miller. Front row: Mrs Rouse, Mrs Butler, Miss Cook, Mrs Slade, Mrs Webb, Mrs Wastbridge, Mrs Fell, -?-.

The street market, market day, Langport, *c.* 1910. Street markets in Langport would have been a welcome diversion for the children attending the Board Schools (built in 1877), behind the trees between the two poles. The Methodist chapel (rear right) was built in 1890.

The Beeches, Langport, July 1947. Earlier the Beeches had stood cheek by jowl with the old schoolhouse and the Board Schools (see below), which was founded in 1827. In 1840 Mr Salway was the master of the boys' section and Mrs Burt the mistress of the girls'. There was once a charge of a penny per pupil per week. The school was transferred to the North Street School in 1877 and the building used as a Sunday School until *c.* 1892 when the All Saints Sunday School was erected. The school building had been demolished by 1909. Note Huish Episcopi church in the background.

The Old School House (see above). It is not known whether these pupils belong to the Board School, which would give a date of pre-1877, or the Sunday School, in which case it would be after that date but, judging by the dress, not by very long.

Cheapside and the town centre, Langport,
c. 1880. This view was taken by Payne, the
local photographer, whose bankruptcy in
1883 helps to date it.

The Langport Arms, whose horse-drawn transport once met trains at Langport station.
This sixteenth-century hotel made extensive use of the local Lias stone, but has Ham
Stone facings for the windows. In previous times it was called both The Inn and The
Swan. This photograph was also taken by Payne.

Cheapside, Langport, *c.* 1920. Points of interest here are the distant horsemen (in army uniforms) heading for a possible confrontation with the motor cyclist, and the window cleaner (right) who would hardly dare to put his ladder on the busy A378 street today.

The Headmaster's House, The Hill, Langport, *c.* 1908. There has been remarkably little change in this area.

Langport Grammar School, from the playground by Whatley Lane, *c.* 1925. This school, the last of a line of schools around Langport since *c.* 1600, was closed in the mid-1930s. The Headmaster's House (above) lay on the frontage of The Hill and, until recently, it was used as a dentist's and a doctor's surgery. The school buildings are now incorporated into a modern house which has been erected on the playground area and which contains many bricks inscribed with the names of generations of pupils.

The Avenue, Langport, *c.* 1895. The Methodist chapel (left) was built in 1890, and by 1906 the Taunton–Castle Cary–London railway line would have appeared in the background.

one mid 1930's

The Avenue, Langport, *c.* 1933. Compare this with the view above when the avenue was tree-lined on both sides from the old Methodist chapel to Kennel Lane. The Somerton road, signposted here as Main Road, which leads to Shires Garage Crossroads and was first known as New Road, was constructed in 1906 when the new railway blocked the previous main road.

Newtown, near Langport, pre-1930. In 1930 electric lighting arrived. Of particular interest are the Newtown Inn and its sign. The inn is now a private house.

Cheapside, Langport, *c.* 1938. The Town Hall was built in 1732. The car in front is standing on the Little Bow Bridge, which was rebuilt in 1875 over the remains of the Catchwater waterway.

The Hill, Langport, *c*. 1895. Aptly named, The Hill climbs steeply out of the town centre and the Somerset Flatlands, towards All Saints' church and Huish Episcopi.

The Black Swan (affectionately known as the 'Mucky Duck'), North Street, Langport, *c*. 1902.

All Saints' church, Langport, *c.* 1902. Langport's parish church, a fine example of the magnificent churches with which this part of Somerset has been so richly endowed, dates mainly from the mid-fifteenth century. There are also earlier parts, particularly in the west part of the north aisle and the openings of the north aisle windows. The tower, again so typically Somerset, is said to be the first in the county to include decoration of its four corner pinnacles by grotesque creatures. The church was extensively restored in 1877. It had been in danger of complete destruction at the time of the Reformation when the Chantry Commissioners recommended that it, or St Mary's at Huish Episcopi a few yards away (they stood 'a burde-shot bolt together'), should go.

Langport 'Terriers' (Territorials). These are members of the Prince Albert's Somerset Light Infantry, at Langport West station, prior to their departure for service in India during the First World War.

The Langport contingent of the West Somerset Yeomanry Cavalry at Langport West station on their way to camp, August 1915.

Langport and District team for the *Daily Mail* Empire Cup Shoot, 23 May 1910. Members are, left to right: H.T. Brown, G.A. Cox (seated), H.H.D. Hemmel, J.C.D. Hemmel, G.H. Hemmel, J. Lang jnr, Dr R.H. Vereker (seated), N.F. Pittard. The team which, judging by the scores on the proudly displayed board, was of an exceptional standard, finished '1st in British Isles' and '2nd in British Empire'.

A comic occasion for charity, *c.* 1930s. Mr E.C.P. Avis (extreme right, back row) was Langport Rural District Council's treasurer from about 1930. Despite appearances, this is not Langport Football Club – there are only nine players. Second from left in front is Mr E.Q. Louch.

North Street, Langport, *c.* 1895. The handsome, four-bayed, Victorian house (right) was once the vicarage for All Saints' church. The local legend that bloodstained floorboards in the house resulted from wounded soldiers being taken there following the Battle of Langport (10 July 1645) is without substance.

North Street, Langport, *c.* 1906. Postmarked April 1907, this picture was almost certainly taken just a few months earlier – the railway bridge (background) could not have been built until 1906. The Board Schools and the police station are on the right.

The White Lion Hotel, North Street, Langport, *c*. 1927.

Bow Street, Langport, with Hurds Hill in the background, 8 May 1945. It was remarkable where the flags and bunting had all come from but, like every other town and village in the country, Langport blossomed overnight with them when news of the end of the Second World War was received. The two narrow-fronted shops and house beyond the Union Flag on the right have been demolished and replaced. What chances of survival would you give the cyclist if he went down the middle of the street in this fashion in today's traffic?

Cheapside, Langport, looking towards Little Bow, 1897. The streets are decorated for the Diamond Jubilee celebrations for Queen Victoria. A stone plaque on a building (left) commemorates the birth there of Walter Bagehot (1826–77).

The depot of Bradford & Sons, Langport, winter 1947. These well-known Yeovil-based builders, coal and corn merchants had depots throughout south-west Somerset, west Dorset and east Devon. The depot closed in the 1970s and the site is to be developed. There was over a foot of ice on the River Parrett at this time.

Bow Street, *c.* 1890s. The street looks quite crowded here, especially with the specially placed (and, probably, specially dressed) group of children.

Bow Street, *c.* 1890s. The muddy road was hardly the place for a group of children to be photographed. Cameras had been around for some sixty years at the time of this picture, but they still caused excitement, especially in a rural community.

Langport Congregational Sunday School Primary Department's entry in the Langport Carnival, 1962. They won the second prize (£3) with this skit of a Gretna Green wedding. Back row, left to right: Margaret Webb, Alan Long, Janet Lock, Elizabeth Webb, Brian Langford, Nigel Lock, Susan Pearce. Front row: Judith Webb, Martin Fell.

An outing to an unknown destination, early 1920s. Mr C. Sandford (driver) was the proprietor of a local transport firm for many years. Among the passengers are Mr and Mrs Hearne, Mr Fred Chidley (with barrel of 'refreshments') and his wife Mary, Miss Dale, Mr and Mrs Aubrey Hale, and Mr Skerrin. The charabanc, said to be Langport's first, has an interesting combination of solid-tyred wheels at the rear and pneumatic ones in front (are there two spares hidden somewhere?), a fire extinguisher and, with four two-gallon petrol cans locked for safety on the side, no excuse for running out of fuel.

Opposite: Langport WI Christmas Party, January 1958. 'The Kitchen Klangers' are, back row, left to right: Mrs Pring, Miss Miller, Mrs Sandford, Mrs Webb, Mrs Hill, Mrs Standen, Mrs Warner, Mrs Pope. Front row: Mrs Andrews, Mrs Davidge, Mrs Fell, Mrs Walton, Mrs Small, Mrs Rouse.

Langport station, *c.* 1900. Points of interest are the plain Langport name board, which dates this picture to before 1906 (see below), and the gas lighting. There is extensive flooding in the station approach.

Langport station, *c.* 1890. The station was opened in 1853 and closed to passenger traffic on 7 July 1964. After the building of Langport East station in 1906, this station was renamed Langport West. Its arrival had as good as sounded the death knell of the local river traffic. The signal box (background) was transferred to the opposite platform in 1906 (see opposite). Tom Pomeroy, the stationmaster from 1889 to 1894, is on the far left.

Langport West station, *c.* 1908.

Langport East station, which was opened in 1906, seen here under construction. The fixing of rails to the sleepers appears to be light and temporary as if the line were in use only for construction traffic.

Dinner dance at the Assembly Rooms, Langport Arms, February 1950. This event was to welcome Commander Kerans (in uniform, centre of seated row) of HMS *Amethyst* and 'The Yangtze Incident' fame (see page 124).

Standard VI, North Street Council School, Langport, May 1928. Back row, left to right: Henry Keirle, Gertie Freeman, Linda Lock, -?-. Second row: Edna Williams, Beryl Denman, Violet Foster, Olive Thresher, Iris Seviour, Prissy Howells, Flossie Lee. Third row: -?-, Harry Wheller, Rose Lelliott, Edna Luxton, Doris Glover, Fred Bennett, Reg Hole. Front row: Jack Hussey, Roy Mitchell, Cecil Cull, Edgar Butt, Archie Hall, Jim Gaylard, Alan Lock.

SECTION FOUR

Curry Rivel, Aller and Hambridge

The Cross Tree, Aller, *c.* 1908. It was at this site, now occupied by St Andrew's church, a mile outside the village, that Guthrum, the Danish leader, and his men were baptized as an act of conciliation by Alfred the Great after the latter's victory at Edington.

Mrs Charles Moore of Aller Manor, a few years before her death on 6 March 1879. Aller Manor, standing cheek by jowl with St Andrew's church, looks down protectively from a small hillock on the parish they both once served. It is hard not to think that Mrs Moore, 'lady of the manor', also looked down protectively on the village and its inhabitants. It is also difficult to look at this picture and not think of Queen Victoria.

Annie Gullidge, *c.* 1925, standing in the doorway of the village shop at Ridley, Aller, which she ran for many years.

The Hunters Moon Inn at Ridley, Aller, *c.* 1925. Although this building still exists, the doorway has been blocked in and moved to the side wall.

Aller Chapel outing, *c.* 1924. Front row, left to right: Charles Sandford, 'Blacksmith' Lock, Mrs Sheppard, Mrs Andrews. The destination is unknown, but the nearby Cheddar Gorge was a Mecca at the time.

Cheesemakers at Aller Dairy, *c*. 1938.

The White Lion Inn (see page 103), c. 1906. This inn was renamed the Pound Inn in the early 1980s (the old village pound is next door). The landlord, Mr W.J. Squires, is sitting to the right of the barrel and poses with his customers who include Vincent Mitchell (the patriarchal figure on the barrel), George and William Mitchell (his two sons) and John Loxton (the foreman on the building of the new London–Castle Cary–Taunton line). The White Lion was a cyder house, an inn licenced solely for that beverage, and, in the adjacent counties of Somerset and Devon, and without wishing to start an internecine war over which of the two counties either produced the best or was the home of that most English of drinks, what better use could you have for a pub? Chateuneuf de Plonk might be all very well for 'Squire up at the 'Ouse', but when you had to do a man's work you needed a man's drink.

Opposite: Aller Football Club, early 1920s. With the Victorian concept of muscular Christianity still the vogue, it is not surprising to see the vicar, the Revd Nicholson, pictured with the footballers, who include Danny Keirle, Walter Leigh, Cliff Luxton, Austin Mitchell, William Mitchell and Walter Francis.

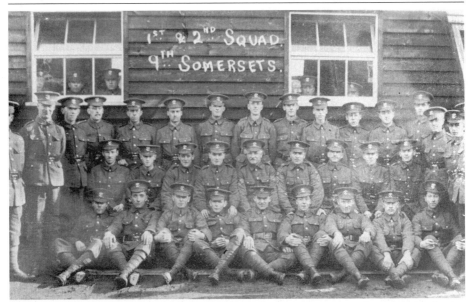

The 1st and 2nd Squads of the 9th 'Somersets', the Somerset Light Infantry, during square-bashing. Those present included men from Aller, Curry Rivel and other neighbouring towns and villages. Despite the laughing faces, there is no hiding the quiet determination that there was a job to be done and they were going to do it. It is poignant to reflect how few came home to Somerset.

Vale View council houses, Aller, *c.* 1936.

No prizes for guessing the 'star' of the show at Aller Court, *c.* 1914, even if he probably had a name as mundane as Dobbin. Among those present are F. Sheppard and W. Andrews.

Staff at Aller Dairies with magnificent steam lorries, *c.* 1921. Left to right: Mr C.O. Hallett (the boss), Frank Harris, W. Leigh, Mark Mitchell, Walter Francis. The dairy, which was later part of the Cow & Gate group, was closed in 1970. Aller Seed Development now occupies the site.

Aller Council School, *c.* 1930. The pupils include Rex and Nora Mitchell, Harold Small, Dick Loxton, Edgar and Phylis Harris, Louis and Lawrence Peppard, Popsie Stacey and Edith Harvey. The school is now closed.

Aller Club, Aller Court, 1900. In the front row are George and William Mitchell, A. Luxton and W. Glover. Club Day was one of the highlights of village life. Men paid a small weekly sum into the fund, those in need (usually through illness) drew something out, and just about the entire village enjoyed an annual party at which the eating (and drinking) and jollity went on well into the night.

Old Cottages at Ridley, Aller, *c.* 1955. The building on the left has been demolished.

The Cross Tree and the White Lion (see page 99), Aller, *c.* 1938. The elm tree had stood in the village centre since around 1760, the year George III came to the throne. Over two centuries and eight monarchs later, Dutch elm disease did what Napoleon, Hitler, two world wars, an increasing volume of branch-brushing juggernauts and the occasional initial-carving sweetheart, among others, failed to do.

The Taunton Vale Foxhounds meet at the Cross Tree, Aller, *c.* 1919.

Home Guard, Aller. Back row, left to right: Dennis Harvey, William Peppard, Ray Mitchell (on leave from the Royal Navy), George Peppard, Mr Napier (a local farmer). Front row: Warry Mitchell, Ted Lockyer, John Lockyer, Mr Jackson (manager at Aller Dairy; see page 101). This picture was taken outside Mr Jackson's office.

Armistice Day service, Hambridge, early 1930s. After the Great War this service was always held on 11 November. Nowadays, with another world war to remember, it occurs on the Sunday nearest, but the 11.00 a.m. one-minute silence is still observed.

The old post office at Westport at the turn of the century. At this time Mr Dyers was postmaster. The group assembled outside is thought to be the Brister family, but the occasion is unknown. Note the lovely Victorian pushchair.

Mr Davis's charabanc leaves Hambridge for a village outing to Weymouth, *c.* 1922. Among the passengers are Mr Simeon Long, Mr and Mrs Henry Middleton, Mr and Mrs Geoff Cleal and Miss Salway.

Chapel outing, *c.* 1914. Frederick Long of Westport (far left) stands by the family business's corn delivery lorry which could be converted (and hopefully swept clean) for use as a charabanc. Today's safety regulations would most certainly frown on the seating arrangements and lack of a safety rail. The ride along the then bumpy roads, even with the 12 mph restriction (though often ignored) in force, would have been even more hazardous.

Gladys Purse of Hambridge, late 1920s. The culmination of Gladys's life, which was dedicated to nursing, was when she became matron of the Princess Margaret's Hospital, Swindon. She died in the 1980s.

Hambridge School group, *c.* 1920. Among those present are Ernest and Douglas Duck, Mary English, Ethel and Harold Paull, Roy Woodland, Violet Cleal, Henry, Lewis and Beatrice Long, Hazel and Lily Lock, Ethel Stephen and Mabel Bunston.

Mr Long, basket-maker at Westport, *c*. 1900.
What happened to the baskets if the horse,
after getting up a fair head of steam, was
pulled up sharp?

Harvesting at Goosebraden Farm, Hambridge, *c*. 1910.

Goosebraden Apple Farm, Hambridge, *c.* 1920. The orchard is being planted for the first time. Among the men assembled for this task are Mr William Gillard (the owner, in the centre with the lighter coat), Herbert Gillard (his son), Charles Dinham, Eddy Ree, Ernest Long and Henry Middleton.

Charabanc outing to an unknown destination, August 1925. Arthur Mounter, despite his youthful looks, was the driver of his father Paul's vehicle. His mother, Florence, is the lady in black standing near the middle of the party. Mr Mounter kept his vehicle in the yard beside the family garage business in the centre of Curry Rivel.

High Street, Curry Rivel, *c.* 1930. Barnards' bakers, immediately behind Jackson's ironmongery, is now a private house. The house on the corner of the Hambridge road (background) is now a garage.

High Street, Curry Rivel, *c.* 1933. Penny's grocers was next door to the King William Inn (right). Later this shop was run by Dennis Symes for thirty-two years until closure on his retirement, early in 1993.

Mrs Jeyes (left) with her niece, Trix, outside Somerset Villa, Curry Rivel, *c*. 1932.

Hambridge, *c*. 1900. It is hard to dismiss the thought that the people here, mainly children, might have been specially asked to pose for this picture. The earthen road that passed through the centre of the village is now the B3168 Ilminster–Curry Rivel road. The Zion Methodist church (right) is now Chuckleprint which, among other things, designs T-shirts.

Curry Rivel Football Club, *c.* 1920. Paul Mounter (far left, back row) was the chairman at this time.

Britannia still ruled the waves – and Curry Rivel's annual fête – when this picture was taken in the early 1920s.

P. Mounter & Son, corn and coal merchants, Curry Rivel, *c.* 1929. Arthur Mounter is posing with the family business's delivery lorry. Judging by the wording on the side of the lorry they were agents for 'Spillers Pig Rations'.

Paul Mounter with the family business's coal delivery cart outside Holly Cottage, High Street, Curry Rivel, *c.* 1920. Note the King William IV inn (background).

Curry Rivel WI on an outing, 1920s. Mrs Finley and Mrs Jeyes are among those enjoying themselves. In those days no lady would dream of being seen on such an occasion without her best hat.

Family group, Holly Cottage, Curry Rivel, *c*. 1918. Arthur Mounter found time during his busy life, first in the the family corn and coal merchants firm and later in the TV hire business, to give fifty years' service (1937–87) to the local community as a member of Langport RDC, much of the time as chairman. Arthur died in 1989. Back row, left to right: Miss Chiver, Miss Smith (both of Ivy Cottage), Florence Mounter, Paul Mounter, Arthur Mounter. Front row: Nelly, Donald, Raymond and Arthur Mounter jnr (Arthur senior's children), Katie (wife of son Guy Mounter, not present).

King William IV inn, Curry Rivel, *c.* 1950. Dart players celebrate a cup win. They include Bruce Martin, Ken Priddle, Doug Barnard, Len Willey and Wilf Cousins.

Burning an ashen faggot, King William IV inn, Curry Rivel, *c.* 1949. This ceremony has been a tradition on Old Christmas Eve (5 January) at this inn for over three hundred years. It reputedly had its origins in the Monmouth uprising and the subsequent Battle of Sedgemoor (1685), which was fought a few miles away across the Somerset levels. Bill Richards (immediately behind the faggot) and 'Trixie' Harwood are among those gathered to watch on this occasion.

Curry Rivel outing, outside Gough's Caves, Cheddar, July 1922. The charabanc belonged to Paul Mounter. Note the 'Visiting Gough's Caves at Cheddar?' board on the side of another charabanc (see page 42).

Curry Rivel Football Club, *c.* 1952. Curry skipper Henry Pope is receiving the cup after the annual game with the Devon side, Hemyock. Also present are Dennis Symes (secretary, second from left), Bill Eagle, Wilf Cousins, Mike Harwood, George Sturgeon and Matthew Male.

Curry Rivel Football Club, early 1950s. This team has just won the Taunton League Cup and are parading the cup around the village on a float. Most of the stops were outside the local inns – this one, outside Symes Stores, was adjacent to the King William IV inn (off right of picture).

Parish church, Hambridge, *c.* 1910. Of interest to the modern generation must be the ivy covering the main church and half the tower, since it has now gone.

Burton Pynsent Memorial, near Curry Rivel, *c.* 1914. Sir William Pynsent, a genial eccentric who, as any real Somerset man should have been, was much in favour of William Pitt's opposition to the Cyder Tax. Although he never managed to meet Pitt, he left him most of his property when he died in 1765. Pitt said 'Thank you' by having Capability Brown design this 140 foot column at a cost of £2,000. There are 175 steps, but the tower, known locally as Burton Steeple, is locked to keep out cattle – laugh if you must, but at least one has found its way inside and made it to the top.

Lang's Hambridge Brewery gets a face-lift, 1930s. Local builders, T.B & H. Pendock, are doing the work. The brewery was closed in the 1970s.

The Episcopis, the Charltons and other Villages

A cyder 'cheese' at Breech Farm, Charlton Adam, *c*. 1945. William Hallett (right) is passing on a lifetime's knowledge in the truly 'Zummerset' art of cydermaking to Edward Jones. It was nothing to see the occasional rat's tail poking out of the side of a cheese, which, according to old timers, 'did give it a bit of a bite'.

Huish Episcopi schoolchildren giving a Morris dance performance, *c.* 1933. Those present include Nora Hole and Eileen Scott.

Customers outside the Rose & Crown, Huish Episcopi (see opposite), *c.* 1895. Mrs Jane Slade (landlady) is on the right and Minnie Slade is next to her.

The Rose & Crown, Huish Episcopi, c. 1905 (top) and c. 1923 (bottom; see also page 71). This inn is still affectionately known as Eli's after his fifty-five years as landlord there. It has been run by the same family for 125 years, during which time there have been only three licensees. William Slade (above) was landlord from 1868 to 1923. The licence passed through his daughter to Eli Scott (below), who took over in 1923. Since 1978 Eli's daughter, Mrs Eileen Pittard, has been landlady at the fine old inn which retains much of the charm of yesteryear.

Huish Episcopi Civil Defence, *c.* 1942. Too old to 'do their bit' in the Forces, many men played a worthwhile role in either the Civil Defence or the Home Guard (sometimes both). Among the Huish men present are Mr H.G. Jeffries, Eli Scott, George Billing, John Morgan, William Tout, Alfred Medway and Jim Gaylard.

Three founder members of Huish Episcopi WI at a 25th birthday celebration with their bouquets, 1950s. Left to right: Bessie Tout, Maude Scott, Mrs Denman. Ladies in the background include Mrs Hewitt, Mrs Harwood, Mrs Bown, Mrs Burrows and Mrs Thresher.

Mrs Ella Kelway, of Wearne Wych, Huish Episcopi, *c.* 1933. Kelway's Nursery (see below) enjoyed a considerable reputation at this time, and still does.

Workers at Kelway Nurseries, Huish Episcopi, *c.* 1909. Eli Scott is holding the syringe.

Boxing match, Langport, 26 December 1908 (Boxing Day, of course). Modern boxers have nothing on this pair when it comes to eyeball-to-eyeball confrontations. Two Huish Episcopi men, Abe David (left) and Harry Wheller, shake before the contest. The seconds are Reg Slade and Walter Hewitt.

Commander Kerans (see page 94), Huish Episcopi School, February 1950. Cdr. Kerans was actually skipper of HMS *Blackmore*, but took temporary command of HMS *Amethyst* at the time of 'The Yangtze Incident'. The *Blackmore* was the adopted vessel of Langport Rural District Council.

Stump pulling, Huish Episcopi churchyard, *c*. 1900. The men faced a hard job winching the tree out of the ground and were probably glad of the chance for a rest when the photographer appeared.

Huish Episcopi School, *c*. 1928. Back row, left to right: George Burrows, Doug Hartland, Edgar Butt, Eileen Bown, Henry Short, Jim Overd, Miss Florence Tout. Middle row: Eileen Smith, Irene Crumb, Maude Parsons, Betty Gaylard, Irene Scott, Daphne Loman. Front row: Ronald Trott, Roy Burrows, Roy Morris, Leonard Brooks, Ernie Bonning, Len Richards, Ken Vile.

Huish Episcopi Football Club, Christmas 1899. Unusually for village teams at this time, all the players are wearing the same shirts, including the goalkeeper. Note the ferocious looking boots, and the vicar who is also with the team.

Outing to an unknown destination from the Rose & Crown, Huish Episcopi, *c.* 1932. Among those present are Bill Brook, Bert Scriven, George Hoare, Harry Bartlett, Eli Scott, Charles Sandford, Charles Cox, Cyril Slade, Bill Perry, Tom Wheller, Frank Lewis and Len Gaylard.

Langport scorecard of a cricket game thought to have taken place on Whit Monday, 1913. Not even an extra! Glastonbury dismissed the home side for nothing after opening with 88 runs. Alby Lisk, who performed the 'hat trick', finished with 7–0. The club seems to have changed its name to Huish Episcopi by the Second World War (see below) and is known today as Huish & Langport Cricket Club.

Scores in the game were:

LANGPORT

C. J. Manley lbw b Lisk	0
P. J. Pittard b Lisk	0
J. Lane b Lisk	0
A. Knight c Lukins b Lisk	0
W. E. Brister b Baily	0
H. E. Cozens b Lisk	0
H. G. Stigings lbw b Lisk	0
H. B. Hamm b Baily	0
L. Parker b Baily	0
H. Weaver not out	0
F. Barningham b Lisk	0
Total	**0**

GLASTONBURY

C. A. H. Baily b Cozens	34
A. Lisk c Knight b Lang	6
G. J. Ingram run out	1
B. Giblett hit wkt. b Cozens	8
H. S. Baily not out	9
H. Baily b Cozens	0
W. Davis b Lang	10
A. Lukins run out	10
G. Edwards lbw b Cozens	0
J. Pompey run out	4
T. Wickham b Cozens	1
Extras	3
Total	**88**

Huish Episcopi Cricket Club, 1946. Back row, left to right: J. Osmond (umpire), F. Tabor, W. Long, A. Jones, G. Symes, E.H. Peat, K. Vile, W. Gabbitas, R. Waite (scorer). Front row: J. Gaylard, D. Hale, J.O. Lloyd, L.H.C. Chaffey (Captain), E.W.F. Trott.

Samuel Eli Scott and his wife Maude Lilian, with their daughter Eileen Mary at her christening, 1923. Eileen followed her father as licensee at the Rose & Crown.

Ladies (possibily WI) in a protest, Huish Episcopi, 1946. The protest was at the government's suggestion to 'eat less bread' after being told in 1939 (see side of lorry) to 'eat more bread'.

'The Harvest Home', Huish Episcopi, *c*. 1935. Among those enjoying themselves are Helen Martin, Mrs Adams and Maude Scott.

Castle Street, Keinton Mandeville, *c*. 1948. The Bible Christian chapel is now a private house.

Keinton Mandeville Church School Group, commemorating the Silver Jubilee of King George V, 1935. Back row, left to right: George Green, Marwood Brown, John Burton, Doug Burton, Bill Green, Leslie Stokes, Jim Crabb, Wilfrid Hodges, Henry Burton, Mervyn Cook, Geoff Dabinett, Bill Burton, George Willcox, Don Atyeo, Lionel Bailey. Second row: Mr Young (headmaster, behind), Fred Green, Jim Keen, Ruth Young, Edna Reakes, Grace Hellings, Madge Paul, Joan Winsor, Betty Dykes, Joyce Pickford, Pamela Tate, Eileen Thomas, Winnie Willcox, Lily Govier, Eric Paul, George Burch, Miss Cannon, Miss Rabbage. Third row: Ernie Willcox, ? Squire, Bernard Chapman, Roy Cabble, Joy Cribb, Sylvia Grant, Muriel Young, Pat Bridge, Nora Cabble, Glennis Green, Phyliss Keen, Peggy Willcox, Beryl Marsh, Beryl Kendall, Mary Cook, Hazel Coates, Margaret Atyeo (last four standing). Front row: Frank Cook, Roy Last, Bernard Hodge, Ken Southway, Gordon Cribb, Dennis Grant, Desmond Brown, ? Calvio, Basil Atyeo, Francis Ridewood, ? Squire, Ivor Wellington, Gordon Wellington, Alan Carter, John Calvio, Phil Cabble. Ruth Young, the girl with the pigtails in the second row, was to revisit the school in 1989 as the award-winning novelist Ruth Thomas. She had won the *Guardian* Children's Fiction Award the year before for her first novel, *The Runaways*.

Bottom of Queen Street, Keinton Mandeville, *c.* 1948. The modern council house estate is on the left.

Quarry inn, Keinton Mandeville, *c.* 1948.

Frank Miller (left) and Alec Cook outside the Old Three Castles inn, Keinton Mandeville, *c.* 1932. Frank was the van driver for Harry Preston, whose bakery was just to the right (off the picture).

Armistice Day parade, early 1930s. The Keinton Mandeville Temperance Band and the local Irving Lodge of the RAOB (the 'Buffs') are at the bottom of Queen Street, on their way to the war memorial. Among the bandsmen are Alec Cook, Bert Alford and Albert Cook.

Keinton Mandeville charabanc at Gough's Caves, Cheddar.

Walter Pattemore, High Street, Keinton Mandeville, *c.* 1925. Walter is at the wheel of a Foden belonging to Mr Robert Webber, a haulier of Keinton Mandeville.

Harry Prestons's bakery (left), Keinton Mandeville, early 1930s. Sir Henry Irving's birthplace (see page 136) is on the right. From left to right: Alec Cook, -?-, Reg Lukins.

Keinton Mandeville Temperance Band, *c.* 1924. Back row, left to right: Charles Wellington, -?-, 'Cocker' Ridewood. Middle row: Jackie Cook, Reg Cox, Albert Cook (bandmaster), Albert Squire, Harry Paul, -?-. Front row: -?-, Reg Cook, Tom Ridewood.

Oliver Chalker with his wife outside the Wesleyan chapel, Queen Street, Keinton Mandeville, *c.* 1930s. Oliver is pictured here not many years before his death at the age of a hundred and was the village's oldest inhabitant. He was both a quarry owner and a farmer, and he lived in Castle Street in the property now known as Sheridan House.

Keinton Mandeville School concert, *c.* 1932. Standing, left to right: David Young, Grace Crabb, Gloria Bailey, Mary Cabble, Audrey Lampert, -?-, Graham Cox. Kneeling: -?-, Ray Lambert, Cyril Pope, Ted Green.

The birthplace (right) of Sir Henry Irving (1838–1905), Castle Street, Keinton Mandeville, c. 1945. Born John Henry Brodribb, Irving was most famous for his Shakespearian roles and was actor-manager of the Lyceum Theatre in London between 1878 and 1899.

Carnival Fête, Quarry Field beside The Quarry inn, Keinton Mandeville, c. 1933. Ida Brown is holding her infant son, Desmond (far left). Others present include Joe and Eric Willcox, Trixie Cox, Marwood Brown, Mr Dyle (bandsman) and 'Cocker' Ridewood (bandsman).

Henry Culling, early 1930s. Henry, who died a few years later, lived in Church Street. He spent his working life as foreman at one of the local quarries and was sexton and a bell-ringer for many years.

Dressed in their Sunday best, a Sunday School outing poses outside Keinton Mandeville Wesleyan Chapel before departure for an unknown destination. Judging by their attire, the date has to be somewhere around the turn of the century.

Harry Bailey at work, *c.* 1915. Harry was a highly skilled stonemason at Keinton Mandeville Quarry.

Grant's grocers at the corner of Queen Street and Castle Street, Keinton Mandeville, 1937. The shop was formerly owned by a Mr Lockwood. In the Second World War the iron railings were to go during a salvage drive. The building was burned down in the early 1960s and never replaced.

Castle House, Keinton Mandeville, 1909. This was the home of James Batt, local baker and Sunday School superintendent at the nearby Wesleyan chapel. Left to right: Ida Colling (later Brown), Miss Ethel Batt (church organist), James Batt.

Keinton Mandeville School Christmas party, *c.* 1931. Among the happy faces are those of Miriam Keele, Evelyn and Doreen Cabble, Molly Parris, Frank and Doreen Cook, Kathleen Willcox, Hazel Coates, Roy Last, Bernard Hodge and Marwood Brown.

Keinton Mandeville Home Guard, *c.* 1943. Standing, left to right: Lieutenant Corporal C. Coates, Private R. Langford, Private A. Lambert, Private H. Parker, Lieutenant Corporal E.Cox. Sitting: Private R. Bailey, Captain Hardinge, Sergeant H. Paul, Lieutenant H. Cabble, Corporal F. Willmott.

Keinton Mandeville Band of Hope procession, Rose Cottage, Queen Street, *c.* 1910.

Garage at Compton Dundon, *c.* 1920. This was the first garage in the village.

Crown Inn skittle team, Drayton, *c.* 1950. Despite finishing as wooden-spoonists in the local league, members of the team can still smile. Those present include Dennis Symes, Bill Eagle, Jim Barnard, Gerald Trott, Arthur Dabinett (landlord), Pete Lissington and Tom Lock (captain).

Compton Dundon Drama Group's production of *Conspiracy of Crayfish*, December 1960. Standing, left to right: Edmund Curtis (the vicar in the play), Jean Saunders, George Evason, Dorothy Napper, Revd Penney (producer and the real vicar), Leslie Taylor, Brian Balch, Patrick Holland, Roman Witcombe. Sitting: Winifred Purchase, Mary Keef, Nancy Hammond, Joan Witherden.

Compton Dundon Cricket Club, *c*. 1960. The club was formed in 1957 and first played at Mr Napper's field at Castlebrook. In the early 1960s it moved to its present home which, as glebe land, was bought from the church in 1981. Back row, left to right: Revd Penney, Jim Coles, -?-, Julian Holland, Bob Moxham, Richard Coles, Doug Green, Frank Vining, Roy Webber, Gordon Holland, Dick Beck, Ted Hammond, Gordon Walters, Edgar Ford (umpire). Middle row: Eric Ford, Les Taylor, Doug Wright, Raymond Ford, Patrick Holland, Mr Shattock. Front row: Pat Ford (scorer), Stan Saunders.

Fête in Drayton Court, *c.* 1954. Among those enjoying themselves are Revd Phillipson, Winnie Burrows (organist), Miss Allen, Major Bowers and Mildred Lock.

Cast of Drayton pantomime, *c.* 1959. Those present include Beryl Lock, Veronica Waits, Roseen Lock and Glen Phillipson.

Drayton and Curry Rivel Girl Guides, Drayton Remembrance Sunday service, 1956.

School Lane, Drayton, *c.* 1905.

The Green, Long Sutton, *c*. 1908.

County council workmen at Long Sutton, *c*. 1905.

Road construction, Long Sutton, *c.* 1920.

Home Guard, *c.* 1943. Formed as the Local Defence Volunteers in the aftermath of Dunkirk in 1940, these men were almost immediately renamed the Home Guard. More recently, thanks to the popular television series, they have become known as 'Dad's Army'. This particular group includes members of the platoons from Drayton, Muchelney, Langport and Curry Rivel.

Floods in the Bicknells Bridge area prevent normal mail deliveries to the village of Muchelney (background). Mr Harris, a postman despite having only one arm, is being ferried through the flood along the Muchelney Road (turnpiked 1829–30) with the mail and provisions.

Charlton Mackrell Football Club, *c.* 1933. The line-up includes Stan Hodges, Lewis Jones, Fred Miles, Harry Mogg and Archie Willcox. Today the club calls itself Charlton Athletic, after another football team from the London area!

Tout stone quarry, Charlton Adam, *c*. 1902. Mr Moody is second from left.

Cement works and lime kiln, Charlton Mackrell, *c*. 1910. The works were closed in the 1970s and the kilns destroyed by explosives.

Georgian Cottage, Charlton Mackrell, *c.* 1922. The building has been renovated and the thatch replaced by slates, but this attractive cottage still retains the old-world charm of a bygone era. Note the muddy state of the road.

Charlton Mackrell railway station, shortly before its closure, *c.* 1966. The station fell foul of Dr Beeching. Left to right: Mr Horn, Pat Carlisle (stationmaster), -?-.

Dedication of Charlton Mackrell war memorial, *c.* 1921.

Sparkford Vale Hunt, Cedar Lodge, Charlton Adam, 1930s. Today this attractive building has been turned into part of the Ron Hodder stables.

West Charlton, Charlton Mackrell, 1935.

Charlton Mackrell and Charlton Adam WI, the Reading Room, Charlton Mackrell, *c.* 1950. Among those enjoying a supper evening are Mrs Daisy Eades, Mrs Kathleen Lock, Mrs Jennings (President), Mrs Kelland, Mrs Nelly Mogg and Miss Walton.

The Charltons (Charlton Mackrell and Charlton Adam) Sunday School Christmas party, 1949. Back row, left to right: Mrs Smith, D. Redding, B. Denman, M. Eades, A. Atyeo, E. Eades, Mrs D. Eades, Mrs Banks. Middle row: R. Hodges, S. Watts, M. Atyeo, R. Codman, R. Banks, F. Crossman, Revd Moxley, -?-, C. Smith, D. Jones, C. Smith, G. Jones, N. Small, D. Smith, Miss Ivy Gwinnall. Front row: M. Hodges, P. Watts, -?-, D. Codman, -?-, T. Miles, -?-, A. Codman, S. Look.

Kingsbury Episcopi Football Club, rear of New Inn (now closed), 1925. Back row, left to right: Sam Stuckey, Hubert Talbous, Len Scriven, Frank Male, Will Grinter, Eddy Coggen, Earle Watts, Watson Male, Mr Keepings (landlord). Middle row: -?-, -?-, Wilfred Engald. Front row: William Mounter, Len Saveage, Overt Male, Charlie Mounter, Eddie Allen.

Rufus and Drusilla Male outside their general stores, Church Street, Kingsbury Episcopi, c. 1922.

The Round House, Kingsbury Episcopi, looking down the Langport Road, *c*. 1920.

A trio of Kingsbury Episcopi blacksmiths, 1920. Left to right: Douglas Male, Jack Duck and Andrew Male.

Petrol station (left), Kingsbury Episcopi, *c.* 1920. BP petrol on sale at the village's first petrol pumps at 1s. 5d. a gallon is enough to make one weep.

Horse and buggy, Kingsbury Episcopi, *c.* 1906. This fine study shows how much reliance was placed on real horsepower at the time.

Douglas Male, the village blacksmith and wheelwright, Kingsbury Episcopi, *c.* 1939. Douglas is posing with a fine example of his craft.

The Buffalo Inn, East Lambrook (between Kingsbury Episcopi and Shepton Beauchamp), *c.* 1935. This inn was closed in around 1957 when the last landlord was Tommy Martin. It originally belonged to Lang's Brewery at nearby Hambridge and was bought, at the same time as the brewery, by Eldridge Pope.

New Inn, Kingsbury Episcopi, *c.* 1933. This was another Lang Brewery inn. It is now closed.

Kingsbury Episcopi from the top of the Methodist church, *c.* 1905.

Wyndham Arms in the village centre, Kingsbury Episcopi, *c.* 1914. The Cyclist Touring Club sign must be one of the earliest in the district. The left side of the inn was later a bakehouse with tea rooms.

Sunnyside, Kingsbury Episcopi, *c.* 1909. Most pictures at this time attracted a crowd of curious children. This one has a face at the window instead.

The Ash Inn, Stembridge, *c.* 1925. This is one of the better-known inns in the district today, but now has the unusual name of The Rusty Axe. The inn was another of Lang's Hambridge houses.

Acknowledgements

We should like to thank Alan Locke for access to his fine collection of Somerton material; Brian Denman for both his pictures of Langport and much help with the captions; and Gerald Masters for many views of old Ilchester. Thanks must also go to the others who kindly loaned pictures for this book:

Marwood and Hazel Brown • Evelyn Buckland • Marjorie Cload • David Gray
Ray and Brenda Haycock of the Arlington House Gallery, Langport • Verdun
Hayes • Jeff Lock • Norman Lock • Keith Markham • Mrs Mounter
Eileen and Royston Mitchell • Eileen Pittard • Ann Smith • Tony 'Toby' Strang
Dennis Symes • Leslie Taylor • Paul Wagstaffe of the King William Inn,
Curry Rivel • Mr and Mrs Douglas Webb

In a different direction, both of us, being self-taught typists with incompetent teachers, cannot speak too kindly of Haydon Wood, editor of *Pulmans Weekly News*, sister paper to the *Western Gazette* at Yeovil, for kind permission to use one of that worthy newspaper's computers.